D1379394

The Missions of California

Mission San Diego de Alcalá

Kathleen J. Edgar and Susan E. Edgar

The Rosen Publishing Group's
PowerKids Press™
New York

Published in 2000, 2003 by the Rosen Publishing Group, Inc.
29 East 21st Street, New York, NY 10010

Copyright © 2000, 2003 by the Rosen Publishing Group, Inc.

Photo Credits and Photo Illustrations: pp. 1, 4, 9, 10, 11, 17, 21, 23, 24, 25, 26, 28, 35, 37, 39, 40, 41, 49, 50, 51 by Cristina Taccone; p. 5 © Stock Montage, Inc.; p. 6 Courtesy of National Park Service, Cabrillo National Monument; pp. 12, 29, 34, 43 Courtesy of Mission San Diego de Alcalá; p. 15 © CORBIS; pp. 18, 20, 27, 46 © The Granger Collection, New York; p. 36 Seaver Center for Western History Research, Los Angeles County Museum of Natural History; p. 45 CORBIS/Bettmann; pp. 52, 57 by Christine Innamorato.

Revised Edition 2003

Book Design: Danielle Primiceri

Layout: Michael de Guzman

Editorial Consultant Coordinator: Karen Fontanetta, M.A., Curator, Mission San Miguel Arcángel
Historical Photo Consultants: Thomas L. Davis, M.Div., M.A.
                              Michael K. Ward, M.A.

Edgar, Kathleen J.
        Mission San Diego de Alcalá / by Kathleen J. Edgar and Susan E. Edgar.
            p.   cm. — (The missions of California)
        Includes bibliographical references and index.
        Summary: Discusses the founding, building, operation, and closing of the Spanish Mission San Diego de Alcalá and its role in California history.
            ISBN 0-8239-5885-X (lib. bdg. : alk. paper)
            1. San Diego Mission—History—Juvenile literature. 2. Spanish mission buildings—California—San Diego—History—Juvenile literature. 3. Franciscans—California—San Diego—History—Juvenile literature. 4. California—History—To 1846—Juvenile literature. 5. Indians of North America—Missions—California—San Diego Region—History—Juvenile literature. [1. San Diego Mission—History. 2. Missions—California. 3. Indians of North America—California—Missions. 4. California—History—To 1846.]
        I. Edgar, Susan E. II. Title. III. Series.
        F869.S22E34   1999
        979.4'985—dc21
                                                                99-19096
                                                                CIP

Manufactured in the United States of America

Contents

The Spanish Explore San Diego

High on a hill, about 5 miles (8 km) from the Pacific Ocean in the city of San Diego, lies Mission San Diego de Alcalá, built by Spanish friars, soldiers, and American Indians in the 1700s. Its white walls, topped with rust-colored tiles, shine in the warm sun of the southern California climate. From the front of the complex, visitors can see the church, the bell tower, and the walls surrounding the mission's interior. Five bells glisten in the *campanario*, or bell wall, which is topped with a cross. Flowers and cacti bloom throughout the year on the grounds of the mission. Mission San Diego de Alcalá was the first of 21 missions founded by the Spanish between 1769 and 1823 in California.

The scene today is much different than it was when the Spanish friars and soldiers first arrived to build the mission in San Diego. At that time, the area was a vast wilderness populated by small groups of American Indians.

Spain's interest in California began after Christopher Columbus discovered the so-called New World, or North America, South America, and Central America, in 1492. Spain was eager to explore these new lands in search of gold and spices. It also wanted to claim this new land and its resources for the Spanish empire and the Roman Catholic Church.

Christopher Columbus reached the New World in 1492.

◀ *Mission San Diego de Alcalá's white-washed adobe walls and bell tower continue to act as landmarks for travelers.*

5

Juan Rodríguez Cabrillo discovered what is now called San Diego Bay in 1542.

The Spanish were Christians. Christians believe in the teachings of Jesus Christ. There were many Indians living in the New World, and the Spanish wanted to teach them about Christianity. They believed that only Christians went to heaven after death, so they thought it was in the Indians' best interests to become Catholic.

One of the explorers sent from New Spain to California was Juan Rodríguez Cabrillo, who, in 1542, discovered what is currently called

San Diego Bay. At that time, the name "Californias" described the land that is now the state of California and the peninsula that we now consider the Baja Peninsula of Mexico. The state of California was then called Alta, or upper, California, while the Baja Peninsula was known as Baja, or lower, California.

When Cabrillo visited Alta California, he met many Indians living along the coast. The explorer described them as peaceful and friendly. He traded cloth and trinkets with them for berries, shells, and acorn bread. Cabrillo's expedition claimed the land for Spain by placing a cross in the ground. After the expedition left, the Indians saw that the cross had become weathered, so they took it down and used it for firewood.

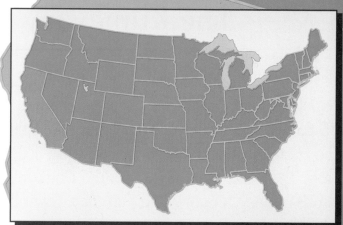

San Francisco Solano
San Rafael Arcángel
San Francisco de Asís
San José
Santa Clara de Asís
Santa Cruz
San Juan Bautista
San Carlos Borromeo de Carmelo
Nuestra Señora de la Soledad
San Antonio de Padua
San Miguel Arcángel
San Luis Obispo de Tolosa
La Purísima Concepción
Santa Inés
Santa Bárbara
San Buenaventura
San Fernando Rey de España
San Gabriel Arcángel
San Juan Capistrano
San Luis Rey de Francia
San Diego de Alcalá

San Diego was the first mission founded. ▶

The Kumeyaay Indians

Before the Spanish came to settle Alta California, the land's Indian population was large and diverse. The Indians lived in small groups of 80 to 100 people. These groups were often isolated from one another. The groups were called tribes. Several villages belonged to the same tribe. The tribes considered certain portions of land their own. On occasion they fought with other tribes over land rights.

The Indians living near the San Diego area were known as the Kumeyaay. They lived in villages near the ocean or the San Diego River. They built dome-shaped houses using bark, brush, and grass they found in the area.

The Kumeyaay had a lot of personal freedom. They moved when and where they wanted. When their homes wore out, they burned them and built new ones. They lived close to the land and always stayed near areas that had a lot of natural food.

The men were hunters and fishermen. They used traps, snares, spears, and arrows to hunt quail, rabbit, deer, duck, and other birds. They caught fish and other sea creatures in the ocean and rivers. The Kumeyaay made their hunting and work tools out of wood, stone, shells, and bone. They carved spearheads and arrowheads out of obsidian, a mineral that looks and feels like black glass. They used flint, another mineral, to start fires to cook their food and keep warm at night.

The Kumeyaay women made tightly woven baskets to store food, cook in, and carry water. They helped gather food, such as insects, herbs, berries, plant stems, clover, grass seed, acorns, and other nuts.

The Kumeyaay lived, fished, and hunted along the San Diego River. ▶

The Kumeyaay made baskets and containers out of tightly woven tule and other fibers.

In the warm Alta California climate, the men wore little or no clothing. In cooler weather, they draped animal hides over their shoulders for warmth. Women wore skirts of grass, bark, or hides. These skirts were made of two apronlike flaps, one in the front and one in the back. Both men and women wore their hair long. Some wore necklaces made of shells or armbands made of twisted hair. Women often painted their faces and bodies.

The natural world was important to the Kumeyaay. They respected people, the land, and all of the earth's creatures. They believed in many gods and spirits. Some gods influenced the natural world, while others impacted human life. The Kumeyaay relied on medicine men, called shamans, to treat the sick. These men danced, sang, and used herbs and other remedies, which they believed would heal people.

Ceremonies were a common part of the Kumeyaay culture. Rituals were held to honor births, weddings, wars, hunting trips, and the dead. Both boys and girls went through initiation ceremonies to enter adulthood. Dancing and singing were important parts of these ceremonies. The Kumeyaay had beautiful outfits that they wore during the ceremonies. All of this soon changed, though. The Kumeyaay way of life was forever altered when the Spanish arrived to build Mission San Diego de Alcalá.

▲
To prepare their food, the Kumeyaay used grinding stones and pots like these.

11

The Mission System

More than 200 years before the Spanish encountered the Kumeyaay, they began colonizing the New World. In the 1500s, Spain sent soldiers, friars, and settlers to the New World. They established a capital in Mexico City and called the surrounding areas New Spain.

The Spanish thought the Indians living in New Spain should adopt the Spanish language, lifestyle, and religion. The Spanish didn't understand the Indian culture. They thought the Indians were "uncivilized" because they lived off the land, wore few clothes or none at all, did not believe in the Christian god, and were not educated in schools. At that time the Spanish believed that Indians needed to be taught Christianity. In actuality the Indians did have a complex civilization that the Spanish didn't understand. We know today that different religions and cultures should be respected.

The Spanish government developed procedures for settling the area. Catholic priests and Spanish soldiers worked together to establish religious settlements called missions. The missions were not designed as permanent settlements, but to be used temporarily as training facilities. Friars, called *frays*, and other religious settlers were sent to teach the Indians about the Spanish way of life. They taught the Indians how to farm, raise livestock, and become skilled in trades such as carpentry, blacksmithing, soapmaking, weaving, and leathermaking. The Spanish also taught the Indians to be Christians. At Mission San Diego de Alcalá the soldiers and missionaries took possession of the land by clearing it for planting, building temporary dwellings, and guarding the area. Later, the soldiers established presidios, or forts, where they lived.

The Jesuit missionaries built a chain of missions in lower California. In 1767, the Franciscan friars took over the running of all the Jesuit missions in lower California.

13

Each mission had a chapel to hold religious services.

The Spanish government estimated that it would take 10 years for the Indians to become self-sufficient in Spanish work methods. It was planned that after this time, the mission lands would be returned to the Indians to operate. The hope was that the Indians would become Spanish citizens. As citizens they would be required to pay taxes to the government. The Spanish called this process secularization. Once secularization occurred, the friars would move to another area and begin a new mission.

Many missions were built in New Spain. By the mid-1700s, the Spanish decided it was time to start building mission settlements in Alta California. The Spanish king was worried about the Russians and British, who were starting to build settlements in the California area.

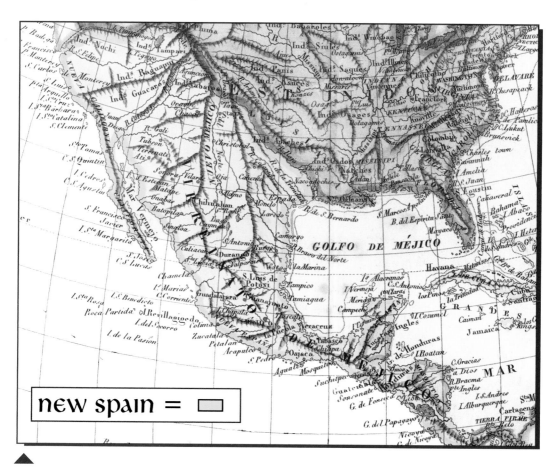

new spain = ☐

▲
This map of the New World was drawn around 1800. New Spain is the area that is bordered by yellow, which today is Mexico and the southwestern United States.

The Founders of Mission San Diego de Alcalá

Two men were sent by the Spanish government to lead the establishment of missions in California. These two men were Fray Junípero Serra and Captain Gaspár de Portolá.

Fray Serra

Fray Junípero Serra was born on November 24, 1713, in Majorca, Spain. Serra, a small man, was often troubled by health problems. Despite his physical limitations, Serra was a hard worker. He became a priest in 1737 and then taught classes in philosophy for 12 years. Later, he worked as a missionary in New Spain and was put in charge of 15 missions there. Fray Serra was eager to go to Alta California because he believed strongly in the Christian faith and wanted to teach it to the Indians living there.

Serra was 55 years old when the Roman Catholic Church chose him to be the president of the missions in Alta California. His first task was to found two missions in that little-explored area. One of the missions was in the south in San Diego, and the other was in Monterey, more than 450 miles (724 km) to the north. He traveled 750 miles (1,207 km) to San Diego despite a severe leg infection believed to have been caused by an insect bite.

This is a statue of Fray Serra at Mission San Diego de Alcalá. Franciscan friars promised to live in poverty, chastity, and obedience to God. The three knots in Serra's rope belt were to remind him of these three promises. ▶

Serra founded nine missions in California during his lifetime, beginning with Mission San Diego de Alcalá. He died on August 28, 1784, at Mission San Carlos Borromeo de Carmelo, where he had his headquarters. Many Indians, soldiers, sailors, and settlers attended his funeral. Some of the Indians took pieces of his gray robe and strands of his hair to remember him by. Today Serra is a candidate for sainthood, an honor given to those in the Catholic faith who have devoted their lives to God by doing good deeds.

Captain Portolá

Captain Gaspár de Portolá was born in 1723, in Balageur, Spain. He was a captain in the Spanish army. In 1767, he was appointed governor of the Californias by the Spanish government. Portolá was given the task of leading expeditions into Alta California to claim the land for Spain. He worked with Serra to build the missions there. The expeditions he led to Alta California included friars, soldiers, settlers, and Christian Indians from missions in New Spain.

The Journey to San Diego

In 1769, five expeditions were sent from New Spain to Alta California by the Spanish government. Three ships set sail northward along the California coast, and two land expeditions were sent through the rocky, desert terrain of Baja California. All of the expeditions were to meet at the harbor in San Diego Bay.

◀ *This is a drawing of Mission San Diego de Alcalá as it appeared in the 1870s.*

Traveling overland, the Serra and Portolá expedition arrived in San Diego in early July 1769.

The friars brought vestments, which were ceremonial clothing worn by the friars while conducting religious services. They also brought other tools and religious articles for the mission. They brought cattle, sheep, seeds for planting, grain, and wine. The Spanish government had given them about $1,000 in Spanish money to buy supplies for Mission San Diego de Alcalá and to purchase bells for the church.

The journey was difficult for everyone. The trail through New Spain was dusty, and the sun beat down on the travelers. There was a constant threat of attack by Indians who didn't want the Spanish to enter their lands. The soldiers wore jackets made out of leather to protect them from arrows. As a result, they were called "leatherjackets."

Portolá and Serra's expedition arrived at the harbor of San Diego Bay on July 1, 1769. Two of the ships had arrived, but one had been lost at sea. Of the 226 sailors who left New Spain, only half made it to California alive. Many became ill or died from scurvy, a disease caused by a lack of fresh fruits and vegetables.

The Beginnings of Mission
San Diego de Alcalá

Founding the Mission

As soon as they arrived, Fray Serra and those who were well enough to work began building a temporary chapel and other dwellings on a hilltop overlooking San Diego Bay. They gathered brush in the area and lashed it together to form shelters. The Spanish hoped that eventually the Kumeyaay would help them construct sturdier, permanent buildings.

The Spanish had many tools, fabrics, and trinkets that were unfamiliar to the Kumeyaay, and the soldiers and missionaries used these items to attract the Indians to the mission. The Kumeyaay watched as the Spanish quickly cut down trees using metal axes and saws. Some of the Kumeyaay wanted to try these tools, so they offered to help. Once the Indians began to help, the Spanish tried to keep them involved in the work of building the mission.

Meanwhile, Captain Portolá and some of the other explorers went off in search of Monterey. Earlier expeditions had decided that this spot would make a good site for a mission. Portolá and his men reached Monterey, but didn't find much food. More than five months later, they returned to San Diego nearly starved. Luckily a supply ship came from New Spain and gave the missionaries and soldiers food and supplies.

Following the procedure indicated by the Spanish government for the founding of a mission, Fray Serra remained in San Diego, blessed the site, and erected a cross. The missionaries made an altar, which is a table used to give offerings to God. On July 16, 1769, Fray Serra conducted Mass, a Catholic church service, and dedicated Mission San Diego de Alcalá.

The modern city of San Diego has been built around what once were mission orchards and gardens. ▶

Once the temporary shelters were built, Fray Serra was ready to found the second mission in Monterey. He left Frays Gómez and Parrón to continue building and to oversee the mission's operations in San Diego.

Mission San Carlos Borromeo is in Monterey. Serra established Mission San Carlos Borromeo after he founded Mission San Diego de Alcalá.

The Spanish used oven-baked adobe bricks for floor tiles, patios, and walkways. ▶

Building the Mission

To build more permanent structures, the missionaries, soldiers, and Kumeyaay gathered the materials they needed in the area. They collected wood to create a foundation. The workers chopped down many trees and cut them into planks and posts to make supports for the buildings. They used *carretas*, or small wooden carts pulled by oxen, to move the lumber to the building site.

Next they made adobe bricks for the walls. The missionaries showed others, including Kumeyaay women and children, how to mix clay, water, and straw together to make adobe. They packed the mixture into wooden molds. Once the bricks were formed, the molds were removed and the bricks were left to dry in the sun. The dried bricks were then used to build the walls. They placed mud between the bricks to hold the wall together.

The mission in San Diego took many years to build. The original thatched roofs were replaced with clay tiles, which wouldn't catch fire as easily. Making tiles was similar to making adobe bricks, but only clay and water were used.

▲

The living quarters were very simple because of the friars' promise to live a life of poverty.

Once the roof was complete, the workers plastered the walls below. Plaster, made from sand, water, and lime, was patted onto the inside and outside of the walls. Lime, a mineral found in calcium rocks or seashells, acted as a glue to hold the plaster to the brick. The walls were then painted and decorated by Spanish and Kumeyaay artists.

Some Kumeyaay began living at the mission. In order to live at the mission, they had to become Christians and follow the rules of the friars. Once the Kumeyaay converted to the Christian religion, the

Spanish missionaries called them neophytes. Between 1769 and 1774, the missionaries and Native Americans built a more permanent chapel and living quarters.

Tensions Rise

Many Kumeyaay did not want the Spanish on their land. The Indians were healthy and able to take care of themselves. They liked their freedom and didn't want to join the mission. Some visited the mission because of the goods offered by the friars, especially the Spanish cloth. Sometimes the Kumeyaay stole from the Spanish.

As tensions built, some of the Indians in the surrounding areas began mocking the Spanish and even other Kumeyaay Indians who wanted to join the mission. In return soldiers fired their guns in the air to scare the Indians. In time these Indians decided to attack the mission. The Kumeyaay's bows and arrows were no match for the Spanish guns. The Indians, who were unfamiliar with guns, quickly learned how deadly the soldiers' weapons were. Several Spaniards and Indians were killed during this attack. The Kumeyaay needed help treating their wounded, so they brought them to the mission's doctor for medical attention. The doctor offered help, which improved things between the Kumeyaay and the Spanish for a while, but relations were still strained.

Daily Life at the Mission

The Missionaries and Soldiers

The soldiers and the friars at Mission San Diego de Alcalá had to adjust to a new environment, a new climate, and the isolation of being away from home and family. Mission life provided few comforts. The dwellings were rustic with earthen floors. Blankets were made of scratchy, coarse wool. The food was often plain.

In the early stages of the mission, the Spanish worked together to clear lands, construct buildings, farm, and tend to the livestock. The soldiers protected the mission and its people from attacks by European settlers and Indians who resented the mission's presence.

The friars schooled the neophytes in religion, agriculture, cooking, trades, crafts, and ranching. They often worked alongside their pupils in the fields or workshops. They were also responsible for conducting religious services, weddings, funerals, and baptisms. A baptism is a ceremony that is performed when someone accepts the Christian faith.

The friars kept detailed records of life at the mission so they could report their progress to the Spanish government. For example, in 1797, they recorded that Mission San Diego de Alcalá had acquired 565 new neophytes and now had 1,400 total. The mission owned 20,000 sheep, 10,000 cattle, and 1,250 horses. In 1832, the friars noted a total of 1,794 marriages, 4,322 deaths, and 6,522 baptisms in a 50-year span.

Life for the Kumeyaay

Mission life was very different from the hunting and gathering lifestyle the Kumeyaay had known before the Spanish arrived. Most

◀ *Both Spanish and Indian men, women, and children had duties at the mission.*

days at the mission began when the bells rang in the *campanario* around sunrise. The bells woke the mission's residents, who were then assembled to go to Mass. *Atole*, a mush made of grain or corn, was served for breakfast.

After breakfast the day's work assignments were handed out. The men were sent to work in the fields, orchards, or workshops. The Spanish showed the Indian men how to grow wheat, beans, corn, barley, grapes, fruit, and vegetables. They also taught them European methods of raising cattle, sheep, horses, mules, and goats. In the workshops, the Kumeyaay learned to make leather goods, metal tools, horseshoes, candles, tiles, and adobe. They worked to repair the

Daily life at the missions was regulated by the ringing of the bells.

▼

mission and construct new buildings. The friars instructed the Indians in Spanish work methods and occasionally worked alongside them.

Indian women made food, baskets, cloth, and soap. The Spanish taught them how to cook in brick ovens. Some of the women still gathered edible plants and nuts when time allowed. They also did the weaving. They were taught how to use Spanish looms to make blankets and clothing for themselves, the Indian men, the soldiers, and the friars.

The lunchtime meal consisted of *pozole*, a soup usually made with barley or another grain and a little bit of meat and vegetables. Lunch was followed by a *siesta*, a time to rest or nap, then work resumed.

In the evening there was supper and prayers. Then there was time for recreation before bedtime. Many Indians especially liked to use this time for games of chance. Kids played a game similar to field hockey.

On occasion, *fiestas*, or parties, would break the monotony of routine mission life. *Fiestas* were held for weddings, births, and other celebrations. The Indians sometimes held ceremonies that featured traditional dances and songs of their heritage. Many friars allowed these rituals so the Indians would remain peaceful and continue their instruction in Christianity.

The Hardships of Mission Life

Trouble at the Mission

Besides maintaining rigorous schedules and going through much religious training, the Kumeyaay who had converted to Christianity and who lived at the mission were usually not allowed to leave. The mission's doors were locked at night. If the Kumeyaay tried to escape, the soldiers caught them, brought them back, and sometimes beat them.

Some of the soldiers were very harsh. The Spanish had trouble finding men to serve as soldiers in Alta California, so they sent prisoners along with other military men to act as soldiers. Some of these men beat the Indian men to death and abused the Indian women. The friars tried to stop the soldiers' abuse. Fray Serra returned to New Spain in the 1770s to talk to government leaders. He was given a document that said the friars could have control over the treatment and instruction of the Indians instead of the military. Even though many soldiers disregarded the document, it was considered to be a Native American bill of rights.

In addition to the problems with the soldiers, the mission had poor soil and lacked fresh water. It was difficult to grow crops, and food was becoming scarce. People were hungry. Fray Luís Jaymé, who had been put in charge of the mission in Fray Serra's absence, was granted permission by officials in New Spain to move the mission to a location 6 miles (9.7 km) from the coast near a river where the soil was better for planting. The original buildings were left intact for the soldiers to use and became part of the presidio at San Diego. Construction of new buildings was started at the new site.

This 1786 engraving of Fray Serra shows him teaching both the Indians and the Spanish. It was drawn in Mexico City two years after Fray Serra had died at Mission San Carlos Borromeo.

Many Californian Indians continued to resent the way they were treated by the Spanish. In late 1775, two Indian brothers began to tell other Indians of their plan to revolt. Many Indians were upset with the Spanish for taking their land, abusing their women, recruiting Indians to work at the mission, and bringing disease. The news of the planned revolt spread quickly among the Indian population.

Upset with the soldiers' abuses, the Kumeyaay Indians revolted by attacking and burning down Mission San Diego, killing Fray Luís Jaymé.

On November 5, 1775, Indians attacked the mission again. This time several hundred American Indians from the surrounding area joined the fight. Vestments and other religious articles were stolen from the church, and the mission buildings were set on fire. Fray Jaymé tried to stop the looting by approaching the Indians. He called out, *"Amar a Dios, hijo"* meaning, *"Love God, my children,"* but he was beaten severely and killed with arrows. A Spanish blacksmith and a carpenter, both working for the mission, also died. Since the mission had moved, the soldiers were farther away and couldn't get there fast enough to stop these deaths. When the soldiers did arrive, the fighting had already stopped.

This cross marks the spot near the mission where Fray Jaymé was killed by the Indians. ▶

Following this attack, Fray Serra, who was now at Mission San Carlos Borromeo de Carmelo, wrote to government officials in New Spain pleading for the Indians to be pardoned. He didn't want brutal punishments to slow the friars' progress with the neophytes. The government in New Spain honored Serra's request, though relations

After the original mission was damaged by fire in the Indian attack, Fray Serra ordered the friars to rebuild the mission, this time with a large church and campanario, or bell tower.

The bell called Mater Doloroso (Mother of Sorrows) was cast in 1894 and weighs 1,200 pounds (544 kg).

between the friars and Indians remained tense for several months.

Rebuilding

Fray Serra returned to San Diego to oversee the rebuilding of Mission San Diego de Alcalá. He also reconstructed the San Diego records that were destroyed in the fire. Once things were underway, he returned to San Carlos and began founding more missions.

The new Mission San Diego de Alcalá was built in a square and resembled a small city. A church was constructed in the southwest corner. Attached to the church is a *campanario*. The *campanario*, a freestanding wall with bells, is 46 feet (14 m) high and holds five bells. The bells rang periodically to tell mission residents it was time to begin their next task, come to Mass, or eat. One of the bells at the mission today is called Mater Doloroso. It was cast in 1894 from the metal of five other bells.

A wall was built around the mission complex to protect it from hostile attacks. In the center of the mission is a courtyard, called a garth, or

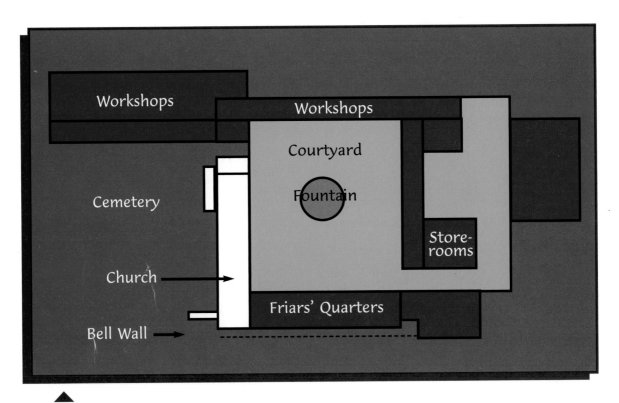

This is the floor plan of Mission San Diego de Alcalá.

patio. Living quarters for the missionaries, called a *convento*, surround the garth. The *convento* contained workshops and dormitories. Unmarried female neophytes lived in dormitories called *monjeríos*, while families and single males lived in buildings outside the mission complex called *rancherías*.

The grounds contained other areas, including a hospital, kitchen, and dining room, and rooms where the Kumeyaay studied or learned crafts. Grain was stored in a granary, and animals were kept in stables or corrals.

The mission residents created gardens and began a *campo santo*, or cemetery, located on the west side of the mission quadrangle. Today the cemetery at Mission San Diego de Alcalá contains the graves of hundreds of American Indian neophytes who died within the mission complex over the years. Beneath the church floor, the residents buried five friars who died at the mission. One of the men buried there is Fray Luís Jaymé, who was killed in the revolt of 1775. He is considered California's first martyr.

Mission San Diego de Alcalá was an average-sized mission, controlling about 130,000 hectares of land, or approximately 500 square miles (1,295 sq km). The mission was so large that *asistencias*, or branch churches, were built many miles (km) away to serve the

The campo santo *at Mission San Diego de Alcalá was California's first cemetery.*

missionaries and neophytes living outside the mission complex. Santa Ysabel was built in 1818 in the mountains about 60 miles (97 km) east of the main church, allowing the missionaries to teach about 250 Indians far from Mission San Diego de Alcalá. The *asistencia* had a chapel, living quarters, and workrooms.

Sickness

When the Spanish arrived, the Kumeyaay were exposed to many European diseases, such as chicken pox, measles, and syphilis, for the first time. Since these diseases were new to the Indians, their bodies had not built any resistance to them. Many died and others became sick and weak.

Besides their exposure to unfamiliar diseases, the Kumeyaay were required to live in dormitories made of adobe. The adobe made the

There were many beautiful gardens at Mission San Diego de Alcalá. The gardens of today look very different from those during the early days of the California missions.

41

living quarters cool and damp, especially in the winter. This caused some Kumeyaay to develop breathing problems. Many of the dormitories did not have adequate sanitation systems. The unclean conditions attracted rats and bugs that also brought death and disease to the Kumeyaay.

Problems at the Mission

In the years surrounding 1800, there were droughts and then flooding at the mission in San Diego. Crops dried up in the droughts, and nutrients in the soil were washed away in the floods. Both resulted in hunger for the residents of the mission.

In 1803, an earthquake shook the mission at San Diego, damaging the church. Repairs were made, but, in 1808, another earthquake destroyed the work that had been done. Finally, in 1813, a new church was designed to withstand an earthquake. The builders strengthened the walls with buttresses, or extra supports.

By the 1820s, some local American Indians who did not live at the mission were frequently raiding the complex's stables for horses. Without horses, it was hard for those living at the mission to keep the other animals herded together. Many cattle and sheep wandered away.

This early drawing of Mission San Diego de Alcalá shows the church with its original covered porch. ▶ To the left of the church is mission Indian housing.

Secularization

In 1810, civil war broke out in New Spain. Eleven years later, New Spain became an independent nation and was renamed Mexico. Alta California and its missions now fell under the authority of Mexican officials. The Mexicans had a different plan for Alta California. Some Mexicans thought the Indians were being treated like slaves and deserved their freedom. Others eyed the richness of the mission lands and wanted to take them over to make money.

In the 1830s, the Mexican government decided to secularize the missions by turning them over to the Indians. Originally the Spanish intended to secularize the missions themselves after 10 years of operation. The friars had not done this because they believed that the Indians were not ready to take over the responsibility of running the missions. In August 1834, secularization laws went into effect in California, distributing the mission lands, buildings, and livestock to the neophytes. However, by that time many Indians had left Mission San Diego de Alcalá to find work elsewhere or to return to their villages.

It took nearly 15 years to release all of the missions in Alta California from the control of the Mexican government. Most of the mission lands never fell into the hands of the Indians who remained at the mission. Local landowners took lands from the Indians or bought them from corrupt Mexican officials. Some land was given away as gifts to friends of Mexican authorities. Mission San Diego de Alcalá was given to Santiago Argüello, a local businessman, by the Mexican government in 1846. Soon Mission San Diego de Alcalá fell into ruins.

Mexico's hold on Alta California was short-lived. In the 1840s, American settlers in California petitioned the United States government

The mission fell into ruins soon after it was given to Santiago Argüello. ▶

to allow California to become a state. American troops began to fight the Mexicans for control of the land. After the war with Mexico ended, Alta California became part of the United States.

Meanwhile, miners who had come to California in search of gold found it in Coloma, California. Thousands of gold-seekers from around the country flocked to the area. Many new settlers and miners were harsh with the Indians, pushing them from their lands and treating them like they were inferior.

California became a state in 1850. By that time, Mission San Diego de Alcalá had been turned into a cavalry post for the United States Army. The church was used as a stable. Laws were passed in the 1850s and 1860s by the United States Federal Land Commission to give the mission lands back to the Roman Catholic Church. In 1862, President Abraham Lincoln signed the order returning 22 acres (8.9 hectares) of the original mission complex to the Catholics.

Eventually the United States government responded to public outcries over the treatment of the American Indians by designating lands called reservations for Indian use. Though these reservations were designed to improve life for the Indians, many were forced to live there in poor conditions. The *asistencia* of Santa Ysabel was turned into the Santa Ysabel Indian Reservation.

◀ **This painting depicts the struggle for independence from Spain during the Mexican Revolution.**

The Legacy of the California Missions

In the 1890s, Fray Anthony Ubach began restoration efforts at Mission San Diego de Alcalá. A religious order of nuns built a school for Indian children at the mission under Fray Ubach's direction. By that time only the entrance of the church was still standing. To uncover clues about the mission's past, historians began excavations of the grounds in 1966. Under the direction of Dr. Raymond Brandes, students from the University of San Diego began probing the soil carefully, looking for remains of the old building foundations. The students uncovered the remains of the living quarters and the library and found various fragments of pottery, baskets, and tools used at the mission. These valuable artifacts help people today piece together a picture of the past.

Now restored, Mission San Diego de Alcalá serves the community as a church and historical center. In 1976, the mission church was designated a Minor Basilica, a very high honor from the Catholic Pope. More than 2,000 people attend religious services there every week.

The California missions attract more tourists than any other historical sites in California. People who visit Mission San Diego de Alcalá can see the excavation site inside the complex. Some of the artifacts are displayed in the Priest Luís Jaymé Museum, which is within the complex. The museum displays vestments and other articles used in the early days of the mission, including songbooks, grinding stones, and religious statues. The museum's collection also features baptismal, birth, death, and marriage documents written by Fray Serra more than 200 years ago.

Mission San Diego de Alcalá has been named a Minor Basilica by the Roman Catholic Church. ▶

The work begun by the missionaries more than two centuries ago has made California the leader in agricultural production in the United States. The city of San Diego has thrived, and the San Diego Bay harbor is a hub of trading activity. San Diego's modern culture continues to show the influence of the early Spanish missions in its architecture and design. Even the city's National League baseball team, the San Diego Padres, recalls the Spanish priests. Schools, shopping malls, streets, parks, and even a mountain peak are named for Fray Serra. El Camino Real, meaning "The Royal Road," connected the 21 missions and is still used today.

Mission San Diego de Alcalá stands today as a memorial to the Spanish missionaries and Kumeyaay Indians who worked so hard and sacrificed so much.

El Camino Real, or The Royal Road, is still used today. ▶

◀ *This is the original friars' quarters. It is part of an archaeological excavation at Mission San Diego de Alcalá.*

Make Your Own Model Mission San Diego de Alcalá

To make your own model of Mission San Diego de Alcalá, you will need:

brown cardboard	toothpicks
scissors	penne pasta
white cardboard	reddish-brown paint
glue	red and green construction
masking tape	paper
five miniature bells	miniature trees and flowers

Directions

Step 1: Cut a 16" x 22" (40.6 x 55.9 cm) piece of brown cardboard for the base of the mission complex.

16" (40.6 cm)

22" (55.9 cm)

Adult supervision is suggested.

Step 2: To make the side walls of the friars' quarters, cut out two pieces of white cardboard, 16" x 3" (40.6 x 7.6 cm).

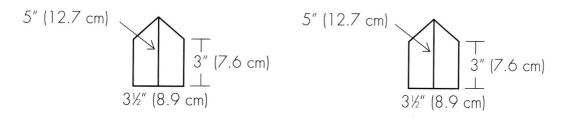

3" (7.6 cm)

16" (40.6 cm)

3" (7.6 cm)

16" (40.6 cm)

Step 3: Cut two 3½" x 5" (8.9 x 12.7 cm) pieces of white cardboard. Cut the corners off the top of each of these to form a pointed shape with 3" (7.6 cm) walls.

5" (12.7 cm)

3" (7.6 cm)

3½" (8.9 cm)

5" (12.7 cm)

3" (7.6 cm)

3½" (8.9 cm)

Step 4: Glue these four pieces together so they form a building. Tape the walls together at the corners.

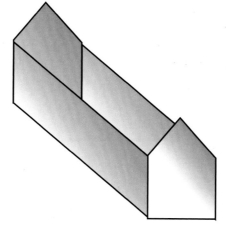

Step 5: Cut a 12½″ x 3″ (31.8 x 7.6 cm) rectangle out of cardboard. Glue it to one of the ends of the friars' quarters. This is the back wall of the quadrangle.

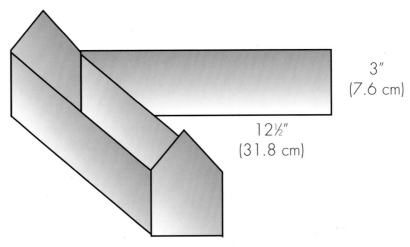

3″
(7.6 cm)

12½″
(31.8 cm)

Step 6: Cut an 11″ x 3″ (27.9 x 7.6 cm) piece of cardboard. Tape it to the back wall so it forms the third side of the quadrangle.

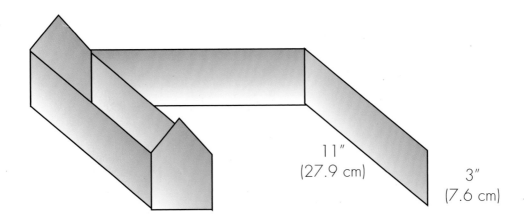

11″
(27.9 cm)

3″
(7.6 cm)

Step 7: To make the front of the church, cut an 8" x 9" (20.3 x 22.9 cm) piece of cardboard. Cut the top so that it has a wavy shape. Cut out a window.

9"
(22.9 cm)

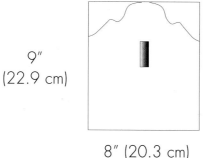

8" (20.3 cm)

Step 8: To make the bell wall, cut a 4½" x 11" (11.4 x 27.9 cm) piece of cardboard. Cut the top so that it has a rounded tip.

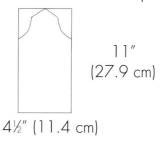

11"
(27.9 cm)

4½" (11.4 cm)

Step 9: In the bell wall, cut out five openings for the bells. Slide the bells onto the toothpicks, and tape the toothpicks behind the openings.

Step 10: Tape the front of the church onto the edge of the quadrangle wall. Tape the bell wall next to it.

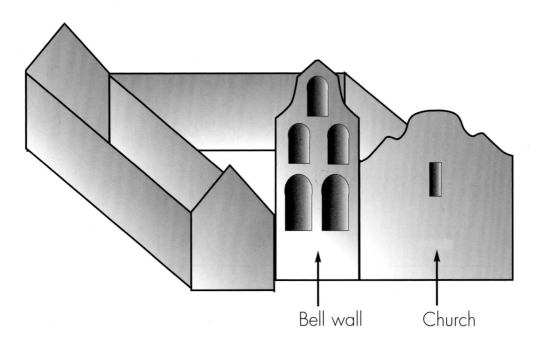

Bell wall   Church

Step 11: Cut a 16" x 5½" (40.6 x 14 cm) piece of cardboard for the roof of the friars' quarters. Fold it in half lengthwise and glue it onto the building. Let dry.

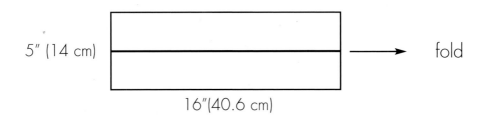

5" (14 cm)   fold

16"(40.6 cm)

Step 12: Glue penne pasta on the roof in neat rows. Let dry and paint the penne pasta reddish-brown.

Step 13: Cut a door for the church out of brown cardboard and glue it in place under the window.

Step 14: Glue two toothpicks behind the church window so they form a cross.

Step 15: Glue red paper in front of the church and the bell wall and green paper inside the courtyard. Add trees or flowers to decorate the mission grounds.

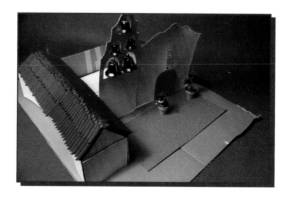

*Use the above mission as a reference for building your mission.

Important Dates in Mission History

1492	Christopher Columbus reaches the West Indies
1542	Cabrillo's expedition to California
1602	Sebastián Vizcaíno sails to California
1713	Fray Junípero Serra is born
1769	**Founding of San Diego de Alcalá**
1770	Founding of San Carlos Borromeo de Carmelo
1771	Founding of San Antonio de Padua and San Gabriel Arcángel
1772	Founding of San Luis Obispo de Tolosa
1775–76	Founding of San Juan Capistrano
1776	Founding of San Francisco de Asís
1776	Declaration of Independence is signed
1777	Founding of Santa Clara de Asís
1782	Founding of San Buenaventura
1784	Fray Serra dies
1786	Founding of Santa Bárbara
1787	Founding of La Purísima Concepción
1791	Founding of Santa Cruz and Nuestra Señora de la Soledad
1797	Founding of San José, San Juan Bautista, San Miguel Arcángel, and San Fernando Rey de España
1798	Founding of San Luis Rey de Francia
1804	Founding of Santa Inés
1817	Founding of San Rafael Arcángel
1823	Founding of San Francisco Solano
1849	Gold found in northern California
1850	California becomes the 31st state

Glossary

adobe (uh-DOH-bee) Brick made from dried mud and straw.

Alta California (AL-tuh ka-luh-FOR-nyuh) The area along the west coast of today's United States where the Spanish built missions, currently known as the state of California.

altar (AHL-ter) A table or stone used in religious ceremonies.

Baja California (BAH-ha ka-luh-FOR-nyuh) The peninsula (now considered the Baja Peninsula) where the Spanish settled missions before coming to Alta California.

baptism (BAP-tih-zum) A religious ceremony performed when someone accepts the Christian faith, intended to cleanse the convert of his or her sins.

convert (kuhn-VERT) To change religious beliefs.

garth (GARTH) A courtyard within the walls of a mission.

granary (GRAY-nuh-ree) A place to store grain.

hectares (HEK-tars) Metric units of area approximately equivalent to 2.47 acres.

hide (HYD) The skin of an animal.

lash (LASH) To tie or fasten with a rope.

martyr (MAR-ter) A person who is put to death or made to suffer greatly because of his or her religion or other beliefs.

neophyte (NEE-oh-fyt) A person who has converted to another religion.

New Spain (NOO SPAYN) The name given to today's Mexico by the Spanish when they settled there in the 1500s.

ritual (RIH-choo-uhl) A ceremony.

secularization (sehk-yoo-luh-rih-ZAY-shun) Turning over the operation of the mission lands to the Christian Indians.

thatch (THACH) Twigs, grass, and bark bundled together.

vestments (VEST-ments) Special clothing worn in religious ceremonies.

Pronunciation Guide

asistencias (ah-sis-TEN-see-uhs)

atole (ah-TOH-lay)

campanario (kam-pan-NAH-ree-oh)

campo santo (KAHM-poh SAHN-toh)

carretas (kah-RAY-tahs)

convento (kom-BEN-toh)

El Camino Real (EL kah-MEE-noh RAY-al)

fiestas (fee-EHS-tahs)

fray (FRAY)

Kumeyaay (KOOM-yaay)

monjeríos (mohn-hay-REE-ohs)

pozole (poh-SOH-lay)

rancherías (rahn-cher-EE-as)

siesta (see-EHS-tah)

Resources

To learn more about the missions of California, check out these books and Web sites:

Books:

Eagen, I. Brent. *San Diego de Alcalá: California's First Mission.* San Diego: Mission San Diego de Alcalá.

Handbook of North American Indians, Vol. 8: California. Washington, DC: Smithsonian, 1978.

Web Sites:

Due to the changing nature of Internet links, PowerKids Press has developed an online list of Web sites related to the subject of this book. This site is updated regularly. Please use this link to access the list: www.powerkidslinks.com/moca/sddal/

Index